HAWAII VOLCANOES NATIONAL PARK

A TRUE BOOK

by

Sharlene and Ted Nelson

Children's Press®
A Division of Grolier Publishing

New York London Hong Kong Sydney
Danbury, Connecticut

Reading Consultant
Linda Cornwell
Learning Resource Consultant
Indiana Department
of Education

Subject Consultant
Mardie Lane
Supervisory Park Ranger
Hawaii Volcanoes
National Park

A giant tree fern

Visit Children's Press on the Internet at:
http://publishing.grolier.com

Library of Congress Cataloging-in-Publication Data

Nelson, Sharlene P.
    Hawaii Volcanoes National Park / by Sharlene and Ted Nelson.
    p.   cm.   — (A true book)
    Summary: Describes the history, landscape, wildlife, and activities for
visitors at Hawaii Volcanoes National Park.
    ISBN: 0-516-20623-0 (lib. bdg.)   0-516-26378-1 (pbk.)
    1. Hawaii Volcanoes National Park—Juvenile literature. 2. Volcanoes—
Hawaii—Juvenile literature. [1. Hawaii Volcanoes National Park. 2.
National parks and reserves. 3. Volcanoes—Hawaii.] I. Nelson, Ted W.
II. Title. III. Series.
DU628.H33N45 1998
919.69`1—dc21   97-8232
                                                                     CIP
                                                                     AC

Contents

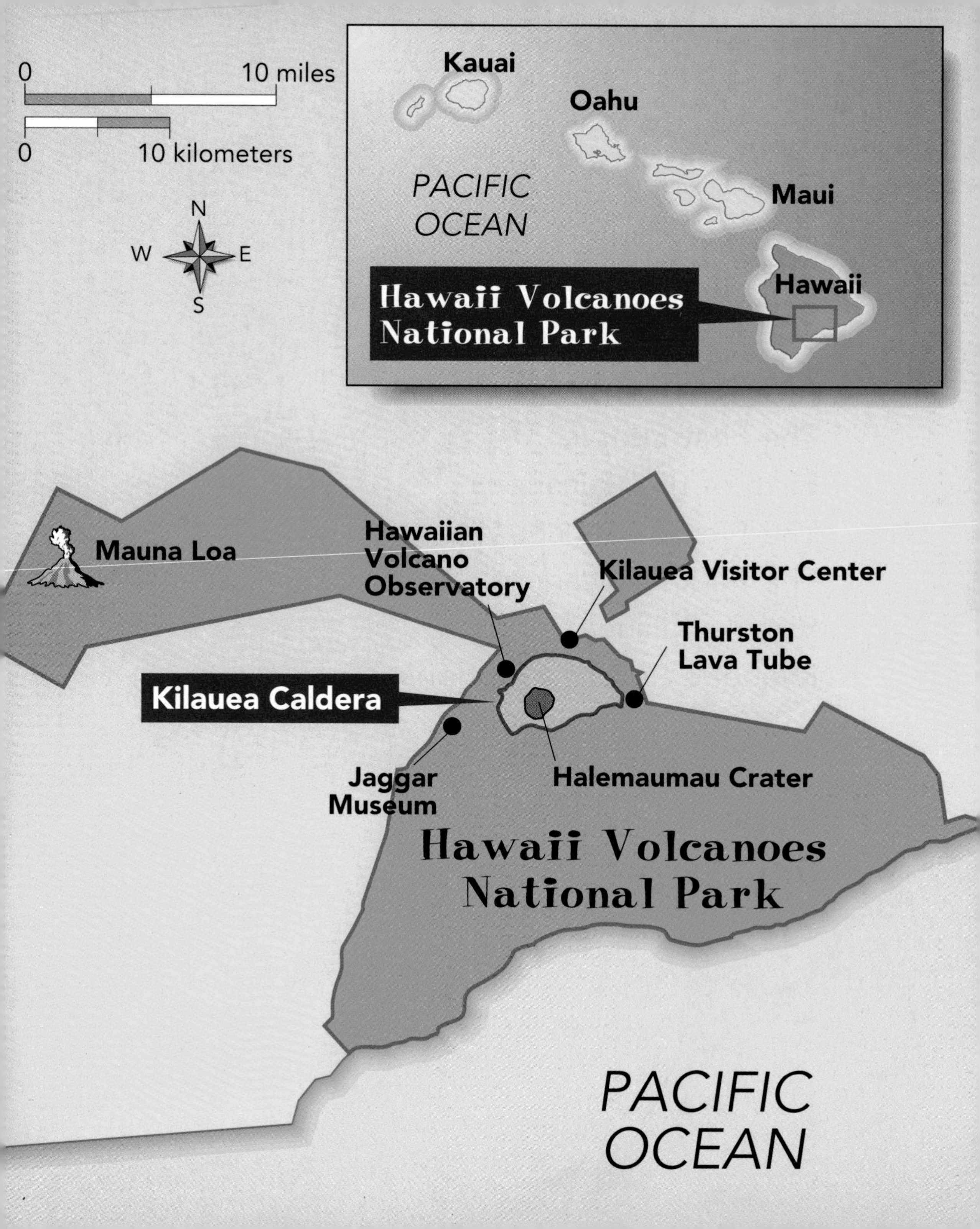

0 | 10 miles

0 | 10 kilometers

N W E S

PACIFIC OCEAN

Kauai

Oahu

Maui

Hawaii

Hawaii Volcanoes National Park

Mauna Loa

Hawaiian Volcano Observatory

Kilauea Visitor Center

Thurston Lava Tube

Kilauea Caldera

Jaggar Museum

Halemaumau Crater

Hawaii Volcanoes National Park

PACIFIC OCEAN

An Island Park

There is a park on an island in the Pacific Ocean. In the park, you can look inside a steaming volcano. You can walk under giant tree ferns. You can watch the island grow bigger as molten rock flows into the ocean.

The park is Hawaii Volcanoes National Park. It covers 230,000

Molten rock from a nearby volcano spills into the Pacific Ocean.

acres (93,000 hectares) on the island of Hawaii. Hawaii is about 2,500 miles (4,000 kilometers) southwest of the United States mainland. This large island, and smaller islands to the northwest, form the state of Hawaii.

There are two volcanoes in the park. They are Mauna Loa (MAH-oo-nah LOH-ah) and Kilauea (KEY-luh-way-ah). They are among the most active volcanoes on earth.

Mauna Loa (background) rises high above Kilauea.

The First People

Hawaii's first people arrived there about 1,600 years ago. They came in big, double-hulled canoes from islands far to the south. The people steered north by following the stars and by watching the waves and the flight of seabirds.

8

Double-hulled canoes consisted of two canoes lashed together.

These people brought pigs, dogs, and chickens. They also brought coconuts and other seeds to plant at their new home. When they landed on the island of Hawaii, they found trees, ferns, flowering plants, and brightly colored birds.

Parts of the island appeared to be on fire. Sometimes the people saw lakes filled with glowing, molten rock. Sometimes the glowing rock flowed across the land. At other times, it splashed from the earth like a fountain.

The early Hawaiians believed in Pele (PAY-lay), the goddess of volcanoes. They believed that Pele made the rock melt and

The first Hawaiians planted coconut palms (left). They also saw lakes that appeared to be on fire (below).

Pele, the goddess of volcanoes

flow. Stories about Pele are still told in Hawaiian chants and in dances called hula.

One of the first scientists to study Hawaii's volcanoes was Thomas Augustus Jaggar. He went to the island in 1912. He thought that the area should become a national park. In 1916, Jaggar and a newspaper publisher, Lorrin Thurston, convinced the United States Congress and President Woodrow Wilson to create the park.

Thomas Jaggar holds a pipe to measure the temperature of molten rock. Lorrin Thurston is standing directly behind Jaggar.

Birth of the Volcanoes

Since Jaggar's time, many scientists have studied the park's volcanoes. Today, most scientists believe that Mauna Loa and Kilauea sit above a "hot spot" deep inside the earth. Molten rock, or magma, rises from the hot spot. When the magma erupts (breaks through

A volcanic eruption can be a spectacular sight.

the earth's crust) it is called lava. As the lava cools, it hardens into rock.

The park's volcanoes began growing over the hot spot

The constant flowing and cooling of lava caused the Hawaiian Islands to grow higher until they broke through the ocean's surface.

about 500,000 years ago. Lava first flowed onto the ocean floor and cooled. More lava flowed and cooled. The volcanoes grew wider and higher until their tops rose above the ocean waves.

Hawaii's Hot Spot

Hawaii's hot spot stays in one place while a part of the earth's crust moves. This crust is called the Pacific Plate. It moves to the northwest about 3 inches (9 centimeters) each year.

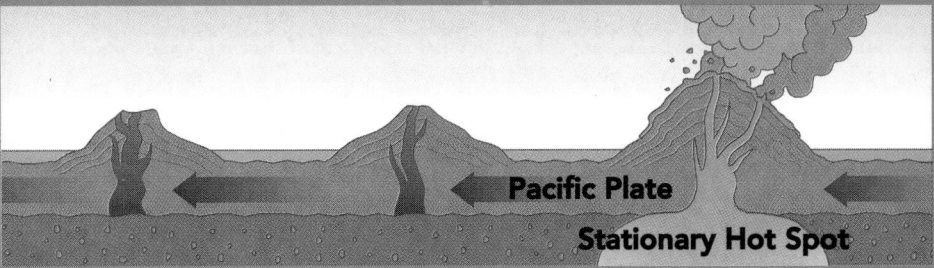

Pacific Plate

Stationary Hot Spot

The hot spot deep beneath the earth makes the park's volcanoes active.

Over millions of years, many islands have grown over the hot spot. Then they were carried away from it. Nine million years ago, Nihoa (nee-HO-ah) island (left) began as a volcano over the hot spot. It is now far away from the hot spot. It has been worn down by wind, rain, and waves.

The First Plants and Animals

When each Hawaiian island rose above the sea, it was bare and rocky. Then, from land thousands of miles away, very tiny fern seeds were caught by the wind. The wind carried the seeds to the islands. The seeds landed in

The first plants in Hawaii were ferns that grew on lava rocks after a volcanic eruption.

cracks in the rock. The rain watered them, and the seeds began to grow.

Over millions of years, the wind also carried spiders and birds to the islands. Some

Although the land once looked bare and rocky, trees and plants now grow throughout Hawaii.

birds brought seeds that were stuck to their feathers. Insects and snails arrived on drifting seaweed and wood.

On the islands, the animals and plants gradually began to

evolve, or change. Today, there are more than ten thousand native plants and animals found only in Hawaii. You can see many of them in the park. Examples

Ohia trees grow in the cracks of rocks.

An apapane drinks from the blossom of an ohia tree.

include a bird called the apapane (ah-PAH-pah-nay), the ohia (oh-HE-ah) tree, and the nene (NAY-nay), a Hawaiian goose.

The apapane is a small, crimson bird with a curved black bill. It uses its bill to sip nectar from the red blossoms of the ohia tree.

The nene is Hawaii's state bird. It has short wings and long legs. Instead of swimming in water, the nene likes to walk on lava rock.

The nene (left) is a type of goose that walks across lava rock (below).

Thousands of nene once lived on the islands. Then more people arrived with their cats and dogs and hunted the nene until there were few left. To save the nene, scientists keep some of them in a safe place to raise their young. Then the nene are let go to live in the wild. In the park, watch for road signs that read, "Nene Crossing." You may see the nene nearby, but you should never approach them or feed them.

Wild pigs destroy plants and can be dangerous to visitors.

Like cats and dogs, pigs are unwelcome in the park. Long ago pigs weren't kept in pens. Now there are thousands of wild pigs. They trample native plants and eat tree ferns. Rangers have built fences around the park's forests to keep the pigs out.

The Park's Volcanoes

Mauna Loa and Kilauea have gently sloping sides. The tops of these volcanoes are called calderas. They are shaped like huge, hollow bowls.

Calderas form when magma suddenly drains away from a volcano's summit, or top. As the summit caves in, rocks fall

A road leads around Kilauea's caldera.

from its sides. Sometimes ash and steam explode, leaving a bowl with steep sides.

The volcanoes are often quiet. Mauna Loa last erupted in 1984. Sometimes they are active. Since 1983, lava has flowed almost continuously down Kilauea's east slope. Nearly 600 acres (240 hectares) have been added to the island.

Visitors are allowed to watch the eruptions from a safe distance. Stop at the visitor's center near the park's entrance to find out if lava is flowing and where to see it.

Kilauea's eruptions sometimes look like fireworks displays.

Mauna Loa, the park's highest volcano, is 13,677 feet (4,169 meters) high. Few people go to Mauna Loa. To see its caldera, you have to

Some visitors enjoy taking the 18-mile (29-km) hike to the top of Mauna Loa.

hike 18 miles (29 km) over the park's trails.

Kilauea is 4,000 feet (1,219 m) high. You and your family can drive around the rim of its huge caldera.

Visiting Kilauea

Kilauea's caldera is about 400 feet (122 m) deep and almost 3 miles (5 km) across. Steam rises from the caldera's sides and rocky floor. In the caldera are large pits, called craters.

One of the craters is Halemaumau (HAH-lay-mou-mou). Its last eruption took

Halemaumau crater is inside Kilauea's caldera.

place in 1975. Some Hawaiians believe that Pele lives in Halemaumau.

You can take a short hike to the crater's rim. There are steaming, yellow sulphur vents inside the crater. On its rim,

Yellow sulphur vents can be seen inside the crater.

you might see fresh flowers placed there by people to honor Pele.

Halemaumau is surrounded by barren lava rock. Some of the rock is smooth. Early Hawaiians named this rock

Some lava flows make a smooth rock called pahoehoe (left). Other flows make jagged rocks called aa (below).

pahoehoe (pah-HOY-hoy). They could walk on it in their bare feet. Some of the rock is rough, like jagged lumps of coal. The Hawaiians named this rough rock aa (AH-ah).

A crater at the Thurston Lava Tube is filled with a rain forest. The crater's last eruption took place more than four hundred years ago.

In the forest, giant tree ferns tower over a trail. You may see the crimson apapane

The trail to the Thurston Lava Tube (above) leads through the rain forest. The happyface spider is too small for you to see, but this picture (inset) shows you how it got its name.

in the tree tops. A very small, native spider lives in the forest. It has a brightly colored "happy face" on its back. It is called the happyface spider.

You can also hike through the Thurston Lava Tube. The

Lava Tube is a dark, wet tunnel that formed during a lava flow. The lava's outer layer cooled and turned to rock. The lava's inner layer continued to flow. It finally drained out and left the lava tube.

Hiking through the Thurston Lava Tube is like walking through a tunnel.

Who Watches

Scientists are always watching the volcanoes. They work at the Hawaiian Volcano Observatory. It is located on the rim of Kilauea's caldera.

Scientists measure the temperature of the lava. They also study instruments called seismographs. The seismographs are used to measure earthquakes.

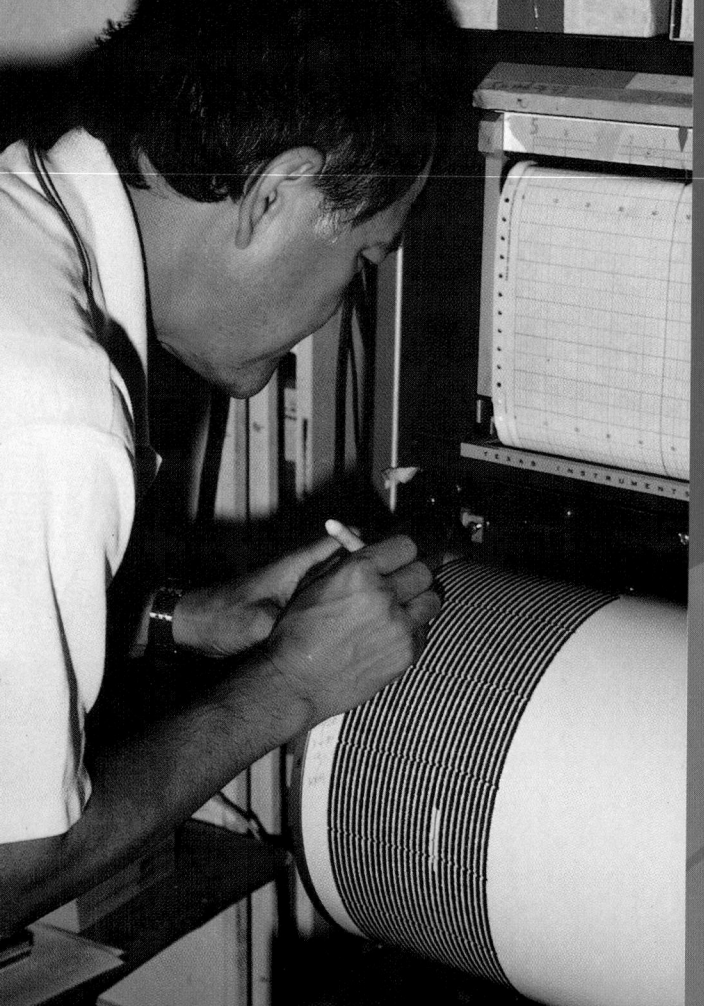

Seismographs show scientists when an earthquake has occurred.

the Volcanoes?

Earthquakes tell scientists that magma is moving beneath the earth's surface. When magma is moving, it means that there might be an eruption.

Scientists are also studying a new volcano named Loihi (loh-EE-hee). It is erupting beneath the ocean near the island of Hawaii. Thousands of years from now, it will become a new Hawaiian island.

Scientists measure the temperature of lava.

Kilauea's Recent Eruptions

In 1983, a crater on Kilauea's southeast slope erupted. Since then, lava has often flowed from the area. In November 1986, the hot lava destroyed homes and blocked a highway until it finally flowed into the sea.

The lava from Kilauea's recent eruptions has destroyed many homes.

Today, visitors can see this volcanic activity. There is a park road that leads to the ocean. You can see steam rise above the waves as hot lava splashes into the sea. At night, the lava glows red.

Visitors watch the steam rise as hot lava reaches the cool ocean.

Kilauea and Mauna Loa will continue to erupt until they are carried away from the hot spot. But that will be hundreds of thousands of years from now.

So, when you visit the park you too can see the fiery events that early Hawaiians believed was the work of Pele.

A visit to Hawaii Volcanoes National Park is a trip you'll never forget.

To Find Out More

Here are some additonal resources to help you learn more about Hawaii Volcanoes National Park:

 **Books**

Ching, Patrick. **Exotic Animals in Hawaii.** Bess Press, 1988.

Ching, Patrick. **Native Animals of Hawaii.** Bess Press, 1988.

Coste, Marion. **Nene.** University of Hawaii Press, 1993.

Fradin, Dennis B. **Hawaii.** Children's Press, 1994.

Lye, Keith. **Volcanoes.** Raintree Steck-Vaughn, 1992.

Murray, Peter. **Earthquakes.** Child's World, 1995.

Thompson, Kathleen. **Hawaii.** Raintree Steck-Vaughn, 1996.

Organizations and Online Sites

Earth's Active Volcanoes
http://www.geo.mtu.edu/ volcanoes/world.html

Giant world map with active volcanoes numbered for quick reference and corresponding links to each site, including photos.

Great Outdoor Recreation Pages (GORP): Hawaii Volcanoes National Park
http://www.gorp.com/gorp/ resources/US_National_ Park/hi_hawaii.HTML

Good information about volcanoes and the life that emerges around them.

Hawaii National Park
P. O. Box 52
Hawaii National Park, HI 96718

Hawaii Volcanoes National Park
http://volcano.und.nodak. edu/vwdocs/Parks/hawaii_ natl.html

What to see and do, trail guides, upcoming events, news on volcanic eruptions, and more.

National Parks and Conservation Association
1776 Massachusetts
 Avenue, NW
Washington, DC 20036

Maui High Performance Computing Center (MHPCC) Photo Tour of Hawaii
http://www.mhpcc.edu/ tour/Tour.html

Lots of great satellite and land-based photos of lava flows, mountains, sunsets, wildlife, and other Hawaiian attractions.

Important Words

barren area where no plants grow

crimson deep, red color

crust the earth's outer layer

hull the frame or body of a boat or ship

mainland the largest land mass of a country

molten melted by heat

native plants or animals found in a particular place

sulphur element that seeps from vents in a yellow cloud

vent opening in the earth's surface

Index

Meet the Authors

Sharlene and Ted Nelson have visited Hawaii Volcanoes National Park several times, first with their children and, most recently, with their grandchildren. They have seen the fiery events and the changes that occur when the park's volcanoes erupt.

The Nelsons have written many articles and books about West Coast lighthouses, the Columbia River, and various children's topics. Other True Books they have written for Children's Press include *Mount Rainier National Park, Mount St. Helen's National Volcanic Monument*, and *Olympic National Park*.